Gran came to stay.
The children ran to meet her.
'Hooray!' said Kipper, 'I love it when
   Gran comes to stay.
She's good fun!'

Gran brought presents for everyone.
She gave Mum and Dad an ornament.
Kipper had some little golf clubs and
Biff and Chip had a keyboard.
'Thanks Gran,' said everyone.

2

'I've another surprise for you,' said Gran.
She gave the children some funny-looking
   parcels.
'What are they?' asked Kipper.
'Boomerangs,' said Gran.

The children wanted to see how
   the boomerangs worked.
Gran took them outside.
She threw a boomerang and
   it whizzed through the air.
'Look out!' shouted Gran.

4

Kipper wanted to play with
   the golf clubs.
Gran showed him what to do.
She hit the ball, but she hit it too hard
   and it smashed a window.
'Oh dear,' said Gran.

Next day, Wilf, Wilma, Nadim and
  Anneena came to play.
Biff and Chip showed them the keyboard.
Gran had a good idea.
'Let's have a band,' she said.

The band made a lot of noise and
 the children had a good time.
'Whatever will Gran do next?' said Dad.
'She's worse than the children!' said Mum.

Gran had promised to take the children
  on an outing.
She said that Nadim and Anneena
  could go too.
'I'll take you all to London,' she said.

'Look after Gran,' said Mum as
  they got into the car.
'Try and stop her getting into trouble.'
'We'll do our best,' said Biff, 'but it won't be
  easy.'

When they got to London, Gran parked
  the car.
'Now we'll take the tube,' said Gran.
'It's the best way to get around.'

There were lots of people waiting
  on the platform.
When the train came in everyone
  rushed to get on.
'Now I know why it's called a tube,' said
  Anneena, 'everyone gets squeezed!'

They went to Trafalgar Square.

On top of the column was a statue of Nelson.

'I wouldn't like to be up there,' said Biff.

'I don't like heights.'

There were lots of pigeons in Trafalgar Square.
Gran bought some nuts.
The children fed the pigeons.
'Oh help!' said Nadim. 'I didn't know that
   pigeons were so greedy.'

They went to Buckingham Palace.
'This is where the Queen lives,'
   said Gran.
'It's enormous,' said Anneena.
'The Queen must be busy with all those
   rooms to clean.'

A big car drove past and
  everyone cheered and waved.
The children couldn't see who
  was inside the car.
'Perhaps it's the Queen,' said Biff.

Gran took them on a boat.
They went under Tower Bridge.
The children were excited because
    the bridge began to open.

It began to rain and the wind blew.
Everyone felt cold.
'Never mind,' said Gran. 'We'll think of somewhere
  warm to go next.'

They went to the waxworks.
'What is a waxworks?' asked Kipper, as
   they went in.
'It has wax models of famous people,'
   said Anneena.

They looked at the models.
'Don't they look funny?' said Kipper.
'You can tell they are models and not
   real people,' said Anneena.

'Who are these people?' asked Kipper.

'That is Queen Victoria,' said Gran, 'and
 some of her grandchildren.'

'She had lots of grandchildren,' said Nadim.

'Queen Victoria looks very fierce,' said Biff.
'I bet she wasn't like you, Gran.'
'Well, I wouldn't like to be a queen,' said
  Gran. 'It must be a hard job.'

They looked at a street scene.
'This is what London was like a long time ago,'
 said Gran.
'A lot of people were very poor.'

'Poor children didn't go to school in those days.
They had to work instead,' said Gran.
'That boy carrying brushes is a sweep.
His job was to climb up chimneys and
  brush soot down.'

Gran went off to look at the Royal Family
while the children stayed at the
street scene.
'Do you think Gran should go off by
herself?' said Biff.
'She can't do much harm in here,' said Chip.

Gran dropped her handbag, and some money
  rolled among the models.
Gran went to pick it up.
As she bent down she knocked into
  the waxworks and they began to
  fall over.

Gran picked the models up and
   put the heads back on.
The children couldn't believe it.
'Gran! What are you doing?'
   said Biff.

'Don't just stand there,' said Gran. 'Help
    me. Pick the models up before anyone sees.'
'Oh Gran,' said Biff. 'I let you out of my
    sight for a second, and this happens.'

They picked the models up and put the
  heads back on.
'They look strange,' said Anneena. 'I don't think
  the heads are right.'
'Oh no!' said Gran.

A lady ran up. She was very cross with Gran.
'I can't think how you knocked the models
   over in the first place,' she said.
'It's never happened before.'
'I'm very sorry,' said Gran.

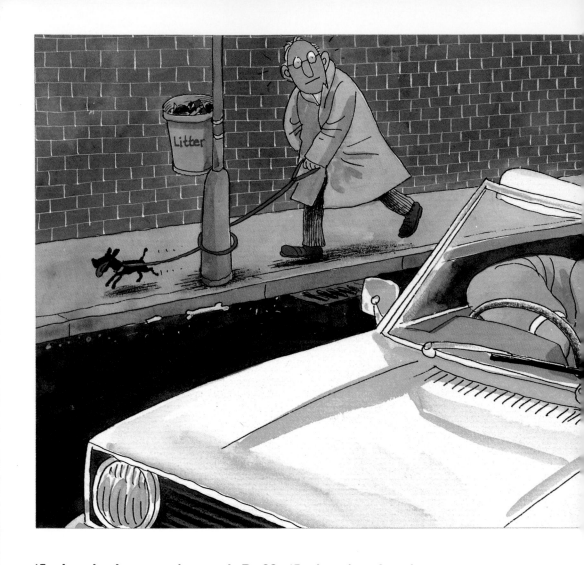

'I don't know,' said Biff. 'I don't think
they will let Gran in the waxworks again.'
'Never mind,' said Chip. 'Gran didn't mean to
knock them over.'

'Thank you for a great day out,' said Nadim.
'We had never been to London before.'
'I liked the ride on the boat best,' said
  Kipper. 'Even if it was cold.'
'I liked everything,' said Anneena.

'Home at last,' said Gran. 'We can tell
   Mum some of our adventures, but not
   all of them . . . and not the one about
   beheading the Queen.'